D1326515

Norman Sparnon

A GUIDE TO
Japanese Flower Arrangement

DAVID & CHARLES
Newton Abbot   London

ISBN 0 7153 8359 0

© Norman Sparnon 1969 1982

All rights reserved. No part of this
publication may be reproduced, stored
in a retrieval system, or transmitted,
in any form or by any means, electronic,
mechanical, photocopying, recording or
otherwise, without the prior permission
of David & Charles (Publishers) Limited

First published in Japan by Shufunotomo Co Ltd
1-chome, Surugadai Kanda, Chiyoda-ku, Tokyo, 101 Japan

First published in the United Kingdom in 1982 by
David & Charles (Publishers) Ltd.
Brunel House, Newton Abbot, Devon

Printed in Japan

CONTENTS

FOREWORD

Japanese flower arrangement has for several centuries provided an artistic outlet for a people sensitive to the beauty of nature. Originating in the mid-fifteenth century, in its early concept it depicted Nature in all her glory and majesty by the judicious placement of branches and flowers in a vase. Over the ensuing centuries it was developed by masters along diverse lines to satisfy the artistic and every day requirements of the people.

Ikebana is probably more popular today than at any other stage of its long history. Its development as a formative art has freed it from many traditional ties without sacrificing the salient feature of that awareness of nature so inherent in its concept. Over the past two decades it has made a notable and growing impact on the West manifested in the many books which have appeared, and the constant visits of many Japanese flower masters to the western countries.

This small book is designed to assist the beginner and the more advanced student alike in their search for a clearer understanding of this fascinating art. Designed to cover the basic and some of the more advanced principles of classical and modern Japanese flower arranging as expressed in the *moribana*, *nageire*, *shōka* and *rikka* styles of arrangement, it is a guide book with a beginning but no ending.

Ikebana is a formative art and like all art forms is infinite. Once the basic principles are mastered and mastered they must be, the student is encouraged to express himself freely in his collaboration with his material.

STYLE: MORIBANA
Material: Iceland poppies and erica.

An arrangement expressing mass and line. The erica has been massed and the poppies arranged at varying heights to inject variety into the design. The poppies provide a harmony of color with the container and a striking contrast with the erica.

STYLE: MORIBANA
Material: Round-leafed eucalyptus and rose.

Six stems of eucalyptus have been cut short and arranged in a fence-like pattern to provide an interesting design of uneven horizontal lines.

STYLE: MORIBANA

Material: Round-leafed eucalyptus and roses.

An open-style "fish-path" arrangement which is made in two parts. This style has its origin in classical Ikebana in which two varieties of water plants are traditionally used. Most schools of Ikebana have adapted the style to their own requirements which usually permit complete freedom in choice of materials.

STYLE: MORIBANA

Material: Green and bleached aspidistra leaves and calendulas.

Natural and bleached aspidistra leaves are intermixed with a free-flowing forward movement and highlighted with three calendulas for color contrast. The arrangement is placed off-center to accentuate asymmetrical balance.

STYLE: MORIBANA
Material: Driftwood and hydrangeas.

The driftwood, expressive of the forces of nature, provides a striking accent for the mass of hydrangeas.

STYLE: MORIBANA
Material: Dahlias.

Dahlias arranged on two levels with emphasis on mass and color.

STYLE: MORIBANA
Material: Australian black-boys (Xanthorrhea gracilis), bleached fern and gladioli.

Mass and line are again expressed but in a different mood. The three primary groups so inheren
to all styles of Ikebana are clearly defined by the tall black-boy soaring over the two crossed shorte
stems and the mass of bleached fern and gladioli.

STYLE: NAGEIRE
Material: Branches of persimmon and calendulas.

The brilliance of Autumn is expressed in the colorful persimmon leaves accented by two calendulas.

STYLE: NAGEIRE
Material: Pussy willow and roses.

Space is utilized to emphasize the graceful lines of the pussy willow which are accented by the two roses.

STYLE: NAGEIRE
Material: Weeping willow, pine
and camellias.
The weeping willow cascades over
the pine and the cluster of the beautiful white camellia "Kamo Hon'ami".
▶

STYLE: NAGEIRE
Material: Branches of lemon and
yellow chrysanthemums.

The spontaneity of *nageire* which is
suggestive of a flowing movement is
expressed in this naturalistic arrangement of a branch of a lemon
tree supported by two chrysanthemums. (See plate 60.)
◀

STYLE: NAGEIRE
Material: Aspidistra leaf, anthuriums and coils of split willow.

A modern *nageire* arrangement using three different materials for the three primary elements.

STYLE: NAGEIRE
Material: Weeping mulberry, bleached asparagus fern and yellow roses.

A double *nageire* arrangement emphasizing mass and line.

STYLE: RIKKA
Material: Weeping willow, Japa
nese quince, camellia,
Dutch iris, thriptomene,
and pine.

Rikka, the oldest studied form of
Japanese flower arrangement, dates
from the mid-fifteenth century.

This traditional *rikka* arrangement
utilizes nine principal branches and
is one of the numerous styles in the
study of *rikka*. Although six varieties
of material have been used here other
rikka styles utilize many more varieties.

▶

STYLE: MODERN *SHŌKA.*
(See plate 72.)
Material: Japanese pampas (Miscanthus sinensis), aspi-
distra leaves and roses.

Dissimilar in form to both the
moribana and *nageire* styles, the *shōka*
style originated from the earlier
classical *rikka* style. Classical *shōka*
traditionally uses one or two varieties of material, however this modern
shōka utilizes three varieties.

In this style the arrangement rises
as a single unit devoid of any foliage
or flowers for a height of about three
to four inches from the lip of the
container.

◀

STYLE: MODERN *RIKKA* (See plate 77.)
Material: Strelitzia, aspidistra, New Zealand flax and golden cypress.

Adapted for contemporary surroundings, modern *rikka* permits a considerable freedom of choice in both materials and container. It also permits a freedom in expression of the more massive earlier arrangements described elsewhere in this book.

MORIBANA

Moribana is derived from the verb *moru* "to heap up" and the noun *hana* "flowers" and hence means "heaped-up flowers". The style was introduced by the master Unshin Ohara early this century and is now widely practised by most schools of Ikebana. Consistent with its original concept it is essentially a naturalistic style which permits complete freedom in the choice of materials to be arranged.

The material is held in place by a needle-point holder termed *"kenzan"* or a heavy metal ring-like holder termed *"shippo"*. The most popular style of container is an open shallow bowl, however troughs and compote style containers are also popular.

The myriad of schools which practise Ikebana in Japan differ primarily in the angles of placement and the lengths of the branches and also in the utilization of the material. Modern Ikebana is a formative art and is therefore infinite in its application. For this reason the schools may be compared with the great fashion houses of the world. The more brilliant the master designer at the top—the more famous the school. However all schools have one principle in common, they generally employ three main branches of varying lengths which are used to achieve asymmetrical balance with a three-dimensional effect.

To achieve good balance, the primary branch may be from one to two times the length of the container plus its depth. The secondary branch is three-quarters the length of the primary branch, and the tertiary branch is three-quarters the length of the secondary branch. For large arrangements the tertiary branch may be half the length of the secondary branch. Any number of supporting branches or flowers may be used but they should not be longer than the branch they support.

As a general rule, it is wise to use two varieties of material such as pine and roses, acacia and carnations, or any other branch material in conjunction with a variety of flower. An arrangement of one variety of flower is quite in order, such as roses, gladiolus, chrysanthemums, camellias, etc. Any non-flowering material such as pine or bamboo is seldom arranged alone. One, two or three varieties of branches and/or flowers comprise the most popular combinations of material. When two varieties of material, such as branches and flowers are used, it is common practice to use the branch material for the primary and secondary branches and the flower for the tertiary.

It should be noted that accessories such as figurines etc., are not used in good Ikebana. In the rare instances where they are used, the principles of the school employing them should be studied.

Finally, to do creative Ikebana which is the goal of all serious students, the basic *moribana* principles must be mastered.

Some of the more important aspects of these are:
1. Utilize space to emphasize form.
2. Be guided by either the container or the material in deciding on the design.
3. Remember the principle of asymmetry inherent in the placement of the three branches of varying lengths.
4. Give the arrangement depth.
5. Endow the arrangement with feeling.

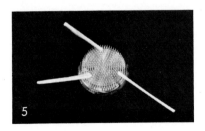

Material: Mauve chrysanthemums.
Container: White ceramic.

1.   The needle-point holder is placed to the left front of the container.   The primary branch which is approximately twice the width of the container, is inclined slightly toward the left shoulder.
2.   The secondary branch is placed at an angle of 45° also toward the left shoulder.
3.   The tertiary branch is placed at an angle of 75° toward the right shoulder.
4.   Supporting flowers are placed with a forward movement at the base of the arrangement.
5.   A bird's-eye view of the three main branches.

6. The arrangement is completed by adding supporting branches wherever necessary but without changing the basic triangular pattern. This is a right-hand arrangement known as the upright style.

7. This is a left-hand arrangement in the same style. The position of the branches of bamboo and small white chrysanthemums have been reversed.

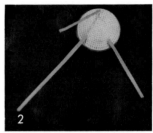

1

2

Material: Mauve chrysanthemums.
Container: White ceramic.

1. In this arrangement the needle-point holder is placed to the right rear of the container and the positions of the primary and secondary branches have been reversed. The primary branch is placed at an angle of 45° toward the left shoulder and the secondary branch is placed at an angle of 15° also toward the left shoulder. The tertiary branch is placed at an angle of 75° toward the right shoulder.
2. A bird's-eye view of the three main branches.
3. The arrangement is completed by adding supporting branches. This is known as the slanting style.

3

Material: Pussy willow and pink gladiolus.
Container: Cream square with green lining.

1.   The primary group of three branches of pussy willow is inclined slightly to the right rear. The secondary group is placed at an angle of 45° toward the left shoulder.   The tertiary flower is placed at an angle of 75° toward the right shoulder.

2.   A bird's-eye view of the three main branches.

3.   The arrangement is completed by adding flowers at the base and in support of the tertiary flower.   It will be noted that by inclining the primary group to the right rear the arrangement has been given a more open feeling and therefore, this is termed the open style.

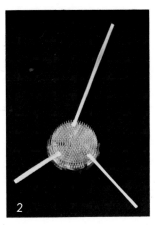

4

Material: A variety of pine and calendulas.
Container: Brown ceramic with green lining.

1.   Respective lengths of the main branches and their supporting branches.
2.   In this arrangement the positions of the secondary branch and the tertiary branch have been reversed.   The primary branch is placed at an angle of 15° toward the left shoulder. The secondary branch is placed at an angle of 75° toward the right shoulder.   The tertiary flower is placed at an angle of 45° toward the left shoulder.
3   A bird's-eye view of the three main branches.
4.   The arrangement is completed by placing the supporting branches and flowers at the base with a strong forward movement to emphasize depth.

1

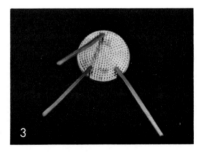

3

2

MORIBANA
LESSON 5

Material: Red gladiolus.
Container: Light blue rectangle.

1. The primary and secondary branches are placed on opposite sides of the needle-point holder with a strong forward movement and at varying angles. Here, the primary branch is placed at an angle of 15° toward the left shoulder and the secondary branch at an angle of 45° toward the right shoulder. The tertiary branch is placed at an angle of 75° directly toward the front.
2. A bird's-eye view of the three main branches.
3. A side view of the arrangement showing the strong forward movement of the flowers.
4. The completed arrangement with the supporting branches added. Leaves have been added to give a feeling of movement.

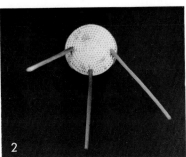

1

2

3

4

5

6

Material: Banksia ericifolia.
Container: Light green compote.

1. The respective lengths of the three branches.
2. In this arrangement only two main branches are used, the primary and tertiary. The primary branch is placed at an angle of 15° toward the left shoulder.
3. The tertiary is placed at 75° toward the right shoulder.
4. A bird's-eye view of the two main branches.
5. The arrangement is completed by adding the banksia at the base.
6. The same style of arrangement using Japanese pampas (miscanthus sinensis) and roses in a black basket.

Material: Gladiolus.
Container: Dark blue oval.

1. In this divided "fish-path" style, two needle-point holders are used, one to the left front of the bowl and the other to the right rear. The primary stem is placed at an angle of 15° toward the left shoulder.
2. The secondary stem is placed at an angle of 45° toward the left shoulder.
3. The tertiary flower is placed in the right rear holder at an angle of 75° toward the right shoulder.
4. Flowers are placed with a forward movement at the base of the primary and secondary stems.
5. A bird's-eye view of the three main branches.
6. The completed arrangement with the supporting flowers and leaves added. In this style of arrangement, a wide open bowl should be used in order to emphasize space between the two groupings of flowers.

1

2

3

6

4

5

3

1

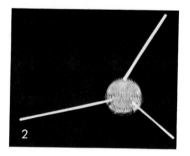

2

Material: Camellias.
Container: Cream oval with green lining.

1. The three branches are arranged in a horizontal style in order to be viewed from any position. The primary branch is placed at an angle of 65° toward the left shoulder. The secondary branch is placed at an angle of 75° to the right rear. The tertiary branch is placed at an angle of 85° toward the right front.
2. A bird's-eye view of the position of the three main branches.
3. The completed arrangement with additional flowers and buds added. This arrangement is designed to be viewed from any angle and is therefore suitable for a dining table or for any low position.

MORIBANA
LESSON 9

Material: Acacia (mimosa) and yellow Dutch iris.
Container: Bamboo basket.

1. The three branches are placed in an upright position. The primary branch inclines slightly toward the right front. The secondary inclines slightly toward the left front and the tertiary is inclined to the center rear.
2. A bird's-eye view of the three main branches.
3. The arrangement is completed by the addition of iris and acacia particularly at the base of the arrangement. This upright arrangement is also designed to be viewed from any angle.

Material: Eucalyptus and pink roses.
Containers: Two light blue quarter-circles.

1. In this arrangement any two styles which have been previously described may be combined to form one composite whole. Here, lesson 2 the "slanting" style is combined with lesson 1, the "upright" style. One arrangement is placed to the right or left rear of the other. In the right arrangement, a rose has been used for the secondary stem and the eucalyptus for the tertiary stem.
2. A bird's-eye view of the primary branches.
3. The arrangement is completed with the addition of roses and branches of eucalyptus. This naturalistic style enables the arrangement to be endowed with considerable depth. The two containers may be the same or of different shape and colors. This depends on the ingenuity of the arranger.

3

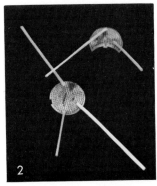

2

1

Material: Dutch iris and thriptomene.
Containers: Turquoise oval and triangle.

1. Here, a slanting version of lesson 3 has been arranged in the oval container, and a slanting version of lesson 6 has been arranged in the triangle.
2. A bird's-eye view of the main branches.
3. The arrangement is completed by adding two more iris and thriptomene to give strength at the base of the arrangement.

MORIBANA
LESSON 11

Material: Japanese pampas (miscanthus sinensis), white chrysanthemums and pine.
Containers: Two grey half-circles.

1. Variety is injected into the arrangement by the use of two containers, one upon the other thus placing the arrangement on two levels. Any of the lessons may be utilized in this way. Here lesson 3 the "open" style is used. The primary branch is placed at an angle of 15° toward the right rear.
2. The secondary branch is placed at an angle of 45° toward the left shoulder.
3. The tertiary flower is placed in the lower container and at an angle of 75° toward the right shoulder.
4. Additional flowers are placed in support of the secondary branch and the tertiary flower.
5. A bird's-eye view of the three main branches.
6. The arrangement is completed by adding young pine at the base of the secondary stem.

MORIBANA: LINE

Line is one of the most expressive mediums in art. It can express many moods such as joy, anger, despair, tranquility, movement and strength. It has always played a dominant role in Ikebana probably more than any of the other plastic elements. It is an integral part of the art of Ikebana and must be carefully studied in order to be able to express its dynamic force.

In these few examples the principle of three elements of varying lengths or shapes, as previously explained in the lessons, is utilized to introduce the student to line in modern Ikebana.

1. Material: Pussy willow and daffodil.
   Container: Black ceramic with cut-out sides.

2. Material: Scotch broom and red camellia.
   Containers: Reddish brown ceramic cones.

3. Material: Peeled weeping willow and white calla and leaf.
   Container: White compote.

4. Material: Dried garlic heads.
   Container: White ceramic.

Although the earlier more elaborate *rikka* styles incorporated mass as an integral part of the arrangement they were generally classified as linear in form. The body of the arrangement provided the mass that bore the many branches exemplary of the style expressed. In modern Ikebana, considerable emphasis is given to mass and color. Many small mass arrangements can be effectively expressed with materials such as sweet peas, dahlias, asters, daffodils or other flowers and foliage which are better known for their color than for their beauty of line. For large arrangements suitable for exhibitions and public buildings camellia branches, azaleas, pine and privet can be effectively used.

The following arrangements are expressive of small arrangements suitable for the home. It should be noted that the basic principle of asymmetry has still been used.

Material: Golden cypress, narcissus, daffodil.
Container: Black boat-shape.

    1.   The materials grouped for arranging.
    2.   The completed arrangement.

3

3. Material: Dried sunflowers and daffodils.
   Container: Terra-cotta trough.

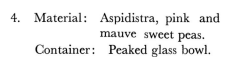

4. Material: Aspidistra, pink and
      mauve sweet peas.
   Container: Peaked glass bowl.

4

The combination of mass and line is probably one of the most popular styles of modern Ikebana. The mass, expressive of strength, and the line, expressive of movement can provide both a striking and dynamic effect.

In the following arrangements the principle of asymmetrical balance has again been used.

1. Material: Scarlet banksia, wisteria vine.
    Container: Black gondola-shape.

2. Material: Oleander.
    Container: Black and terra-cotta gondola-shapes.

1

2

3. Material: Tangle daisy, red and white
   sweet peas.
   Container: Light green with cut-out
   sides.

4. Material: Pussy willow, golden cypress and calendulas.
   Container: Triple bowl terra-cotta.

Classical arrangements are expressed in any of three styles known as "*shin*", "*gyō*" and "*sō*". Sometimes referred to as "formal", "semi-formal" and "informal" they are more correctly rendered as straight, semi-cursive and cursive. *Shin*, literally meaning "true" denotes a feeling of straightness or perpendicularity. An arrangement done in the *shin* style is slender and upright and this style permeates Ikebana generally.

The following arrangements exemplify this style in modern Ikebana.

1. Material: Scotch broom and small yellow chrysanthemums.
   Container: Black ceramic.

2. Material: Lotus pod, furled lotus leaf and red ginger.
   Container: Two black metal bowls.

3. Material: Bamboo leaves sprayed black, and yellow chrysanthemums.
    Container: Cut-out bamboo.

4. Material: Lotus pods and white chrysanthemums.
    Container: Brown and black ceramic.

MORIBANA: DOUBLE SHIN

"Double-*shin*" has its origin in *rikka* in which it is one of the traditional *rikka* arrangements. It employs two *shin* branches of equal height which gives the impression of one arrangement split down the middle. In modern Ikebana it is used merely as an idea for free expression.

1. Material: Young pine, bamboo and white chrysanthemums.
    Container: Yellow glass.

2. Material: Cat-tails and dried cat-tail grass.
    Container: Brown ceramic.

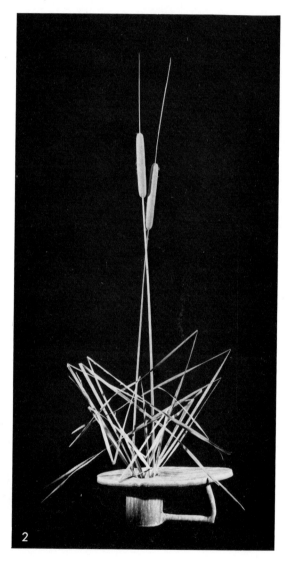

MORIBANA: DOUBLE SHIN

3. Material: White callas and leaf, acacia
   and aspidistra leaf.
   Container: Turquoise trough.

4. Material: Red hot pokers (kniphofia)
   and fern.
   Container: Terra-cotta bowl.

Utilizing the basic principles of asymmetry and the third dimension both of which form an integral part of the study of Ikebana, the student is encouraged to express himself spontaneously and freely in collaboration with his material.

The following arrangements are styles which have been freely expressed within the framework of the basic principles.

1. Material: Camellias.
    Container: Red peaked bowl.

2. Material: Weeping willow, pine and camellias.
    Container: Brown ceramic lined with green.

3. Material: Pine, bamboo and white chrysanthemums.
    Container: Orange bowl.

4. Material: New Zealand flax and dark red chrysanthemums.
    Container: Black and tan bowl.

5. Material: Strelitzia and leaf, papyrus.
    Container: Tan compote.

6. Material: Aspidistra leaves and white
                 chrysanthemums.
    Container: White trough.

7. Material: Anthurium and leaves.
    Container: Green and white boat-shape

8. Material: Edgeworthia papyrifera and
                 roses.
    Container: Black gondola-shape.

6

7

8

9

9. Material: Pine, bamboo and yellow roses.
   Container: Terra-cotta compote.

10. Material: Pussy willow and cream stock.
    Container: Black basket.

11. Material: Pussy willow and camellias.
    Container: Two-level black ceramic.

12. Material: Yellow chrysanthemums, sunflow
    er and crataegus berries.
    Container: Orange trough.

12

MORIBANA: FREE EXPRESSION

10

11

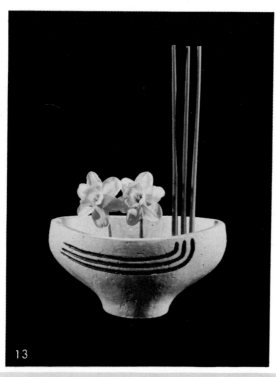

13

13. Material: Daffodils.
    Container: White with black stripes.

14. Material: Narcissus.
    Containers: Two red half-circles.

14

15

15. Material: Weeping willow and red
tulips.
Container: Green bowl.

16. Material: Yellow bachelor buttons
and scarlet Christmas bells.
Container: Terra-cotta bowl.

16

MORIMONO

Morimono from the compound *moru* "to heap up" and *mono*, "things" hence "heaped-up things". It is an arrangement of any combination of fruit, vegetables, or fruit and vegetables with or without flowers.

The arrangement may be made on a plate or any shallow dish, basket, leaf or any flat base which is in harmony with the material to be arranged.

1. Material: Fruit and vegetables, pine and camellia.
    Container: Red lacquer plate.

2. Material: Fruit and camellia.
    Container: Bamboo basket.

FLOATING (UKI-BANA)

Uki-bana, meaning floating flowers, is an arrangement of flowers or foliage floating in a shallow dish.   Here also, the principle of asymmetry is used.

1.   Material: Camellias and asparagus fern.
    Container: Black lacquer plate.

2.   Material: Variegated geranium leaves and florets of white gladiolus.
    Container: Green glass bowl.

Nageire is derived from the verb *nage-ireru* meaning "to throw (fling) into" and hence has a spontaneous casual feeling.   It is one of the oldest and most beautiful styles of Ikebana.

Nageire features a tall container and employs various artifices to hold the branches in position.   For good balance, the length of the primary branch may be from one to two times the height plus the width of the container.   The secondary branch is three-quarters the length of the primary branch and the tertiary branch is three-quarters the length of the secondary branch.   For large arrangements, the tertiary branch may be one-half the length of the secondary branch.

The following illustrations depict some of the most common methods used to hold the branches in position.

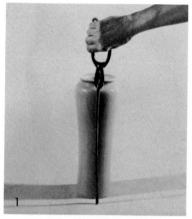

1.   Cut a vertical stick the height of the container and split it with the scissors for a distance of about 2 or 3 inches.

2.   Hold the branch in the vase in the position you wish it to hold in the completed arrangement.

3.   Split the stem with a vertical cut for about 2 or 3 inches.

4.   Join the stems by placing one inside the other.

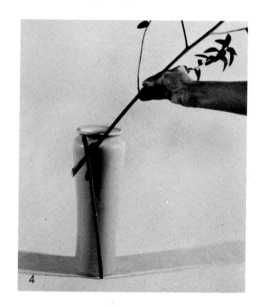

5   6

5. For square or round vases with straight sides. Cut two short sticks and criss-cross them about three-quarters of an inch down from the mouth of the container.
6. Place the branch or flower in one of the quadrants and lean the end of the branch against the wall of the vase. Cut the branch on the slant so it will grip the wall of the container.

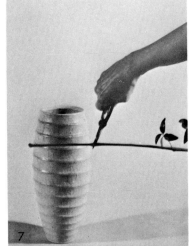

7   8

9   10

7. For bulbous vases, the down stick may be used, or cut a stick the width of the vase at a spot about four inches down from the mouth of the container.
8. Split the branch horizontally for a distance of about 2 or 3 inches and place the short stick into the cut.
9. Scissor the branch and its cross-piece to place them into the vase and then revert the cross-piece to its horizontal position so that the weight of the branch will cause the cross-piece to grip the inside of the neck of the vase.
10. The branch in position.

Material: Branch of lemon tree and yellow chrysanthemums.
Container: Brown ceramic. (See color plate 14.)

1. The respective lengths of the branches. The primary branch is shown with its extension attached.
2. Close-up of the method of attaching the vertical extension to the primary branch.
3. The primary branch is placed in a slanting position in the vase and leans to the left front.
4. The arrangement is completed by adding the lemon and the two chrysanthemums.

Material: Japanese pampas (miscanthus sinensis) and small white chrysanthemums.
Container: Brown basket.

1. The primary stems of pampas are placed in the basket at an angle of 15° toward the left shoulder.
2. The tertiary group of chrysanthemums are arranged at an angle of 75° toward the right shoulder.
3. The method of holding the stems in position in the basket is clearly shown.
4. The arrangement is completed by placing chrysanthemums at the mouth of the container. In this style no secondary group of stems has been used.

Material: Pine and carnations.
Container: White ceramic vase and bowl.

A composite arrangement of a *moribana* and a *nageire* provides one of the popular Ikebana styles. Although each arrangement is complete within itself, the two must be constructed to provide one harmonious whole. In the arrangement illustrated, a cascading *nageire* is combined with the *moribana*.

1. The positions of the three main stems of each arrangement are clearly shown.

2. The arrangement is completed by adding carnations to each component. Here the *nageire* stands to the right rear of the *moribana*, however it may be placed to the left rear or to the left or right front. This is dictated by the location of the arrangement and by the type of material used.

1. Material: Camellias.
   Container: White ceramic.

2. Material: Camellias.
   Container: Gourd.

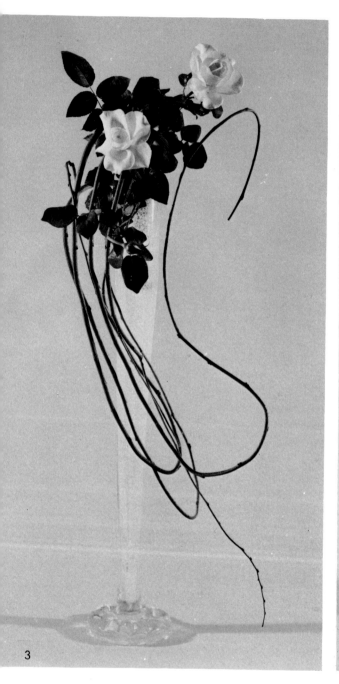

3. Material: White roses and weeping mulberry.
   Container: Tall white glass.

4. Material: Anthurium and leaf.
   Container: Orange ceramic.

SHŌKA

The word *shōka* is derived from the compound meaning "living flowers" which may also be read, *seika* or Ikebana. It is one of the oldest styles of Ikebana which developed from the *rikka* style early in the eighteenth century. Like the *moribana* style, it employs three principal branches but differs from a *moribana* arrangement on one important point. Irrespective of the number of branches used they rise from the mouth of the container as a single unit and devoid of any foliage for a height of from three to four inches.

Classical *shōka* is renowned for its elegant linear style arrangements of one or two varieties of material such as the aspidistra, chrysanthemums, narcissus, iris, and the pine and chrysanthemum. Although modern *shōka* commonly uses three varieties of material, classical *shōka* seldom uses more than two varieties of branches and flowers.

The branches are traditionally held in position by a forked twig aided by a cross-bar. However in modern *shōka* a needle-point holder is commonly used.

For good balance, the length of the primary branch may be from one and a half to three times the height or width of the container. The secondary branch is two-thirds of the length of the primary branch and the tertiary is one-third of the length of the primary branch.

When flowers are combined with branches, the branch material is used for the primary and secondary stems and the flowers are used for the tertiary placement. This tertiary grouping is known as the *nejime*.

Modern *shōka* was developed to meet the requirements of contemporary living and permits great freedom in the choice and combination of both materials and containers. The classical theme is used as a basis for free expression.

Material: Aspidistra.
Container: Bamboo.

1. The five leaves showing their respective lengths and from right to left their order of placement in the forked twig. The curved leaf on the right is the tertiary leaf. Next to it is the leaf which is placed to the front of the primary leaf. The tall leaf in the center is the primary leaf. Next, is the leaf which is placed to the back of the primary leaf. The leaf on the left is the secondary leaf. The white dot indicates the wide side of the leaf when viewed from the back. It will be noted that the primary, the leaf to be placed to the front of the primary and the tertiary leaf are all wide left of the center vein. The leaf to be placed to the back of the primary and the secondary leaf are wide right of the center vein.

2. The completed arrangement showing the position of the wide sides of the leaves. The two leaves at the top right and mid-left are placed to the back of the primary leaf which is the central axis. They are arranged with the front of the leaf facing the viewer. Hence the wide side of the leaf is left of the center vein. The primary leaf, the tertiary leaf on the lower right, and the leaf between these two leaves are arranged with the backs of the leaves facing the viewer. Thus the wide side of the leaf appears on the left of the center vein.

3. The forked twig in position in the bamboo container. The branches are placed in the crutch of the fork and then wedged into position by placing the cross-bar at the back of the branches.

4. The completed arrangement. The tall primary leaf stands with its back to the viewer and with its tip in line with its base. The tip of the leaf is turned slightly to show its front. The secondary leaf on the mid-left and the tertiary leaf on the lower right, face the primary leaf. The leaf at the back of the primary leaf on the upper right, and the leaf to the front of the primary leaf at the center front, also face the primary leaf. In this way the five leaves are in perfect harmony with each other, displaying a balance of the positive and negative aspects of the leaves.

SHÔKA
LESSON 17

Material: Pine and chrysanthemums.
Container: Green compote.

1.   The tertiary group of chrysanthemums and the branch of pine are placed in position in the needle-point holder.
2.   The primary branch and the branch to the back of the primary branch, are added.
3.   The arrangement is completed by adding the secondary branch and its support.

SHÔKA
LESSON 18

Material: White gladiolus.
Container: White trough.

1. The component parts and their respective lengths.
2. The primary branch is placed in position. It curves slightly to the left with its tip over its base.
3. A leaf is added to the back of the primary, and the secondary group of two leaves is arranged on the left.
4. The arrangement is completed by adding the tertiary flower and the two leaves on the lower right.

4

2

3

Material: Strelitzia.
Container: Brown trough.

1. The tertiary grouping of two leaves and a flower is placed in position. The two leaves embrace the flower.
2. The primary group of two leaves and a flower is added. The two leaves are arranged with their backs to the viewer.
3. The secondary leaf is added to complete the arrangement. This leaf faces the primary leaf.

Material: Molucca balm, cypress and pink carnations.
Container: Black and white bowl.

1. Respective lengths of the branches.
2. The primary branch in position.
3. The "body" of cypress is added, supported by the two carnations.
4. The tertiary stem of molucca balm is added on the lower right and a supporting branch to give balance is added on the lower left.

This style is a modern *shōka*.

Material: Japanese pampas, aspidistra and yellow roses.
Container: Blue and white compote. (See color plate 18.)

1. The respective lengths of the branches.
2. The primary branch supported by one branch to its front and one to the rear.
3. The secondary stem of an aspidistra leaf, half of which has been shredded, is added.
4. The tertiary grouping of roses and aspidistra leaf is added to complete the arrangement.

This style is a modern *shōka*.

1. Material: Five chrysanthe-
                mums.
    Container: Grey ceramic.

2. Material: Pussy willow, erica
                and yellow Dutch
                iris.
    Container: Dark blue ceramic.

RIKKA

Rikka meaning "standing flowers" is the oldest studied form of Japanese flower arrangement. It had its origin in the mid-fifteenth century and in its original concept depicted nature in all her glory and grandeur. For several hundred years this style of arrangement reigned supreme and was usually engaged in by the warrior class, the Japanese nobility and the Buddhist priests. The arrangements were usually large, elegant and magnificent, at times being massive in their proportions. They were beautifully balanced and called for considerable skill on the part of the arranger.

In its original concept a *rikka* symbolized the sacred Mount Meru of the Hindu and Buddhist cosmology. Over the ensuing years principles of *rikka* were formulated and nine principal branches were established. Early in the eighteenth century the three-branch *shōka* style was developed from the *rikka* and this new style supplanted the *rikka* in popularity. However, during the last decade there has been a *rikka* renaissance and this once revered style of Ikebana is again being studied and practised widely throughout Japan.

An average *rikka* measures approximately from three to five times the height or width of the container. Once the length of the primary branch has been decided, all other branches are balanced according to a set pattern of measurements. These measurements can be approximately gauged when it is realized that a completed *rikka* is globular in form and hence has great depth. An understanding of its balance and construction may be grasped from the following lesson.

Material: Pussy willow, strelitzia leaves, tuberose, asparagus fern, anthurium leaf, aspidistra leaf, roses.
Container: Dark blue pot.

. The primary stem of pussy willow stands erect with its tip over its base. It is supported by a stem to its left front and a stem to its right rear which also serves as the "overhanging" branch.
. The two secondary branches are added to the left rear.
. The tertiary or "flowing" branch is added to the right front. These three branches constitute the basic pattern of most styles of Ikebana.
. Two leaves are added. The "receiving" branch on the right rear, and the "waiting" branch on the lower left.
. The "straight" stem of tuberose is added.
. The "body" of asparagus fern is added.
. The arrangement is completed by adding the "anterior" anthurium leaf to the lower front and by placing roses in the upper right and lower left of the "body". The "rear wall" consisting of an aspidistra leaf is placed to the rear of the "body".

This is a simple *rikka* in which although all nine branches have been employed, a minimum of material has been used.

Material: Strelitzia flower and leaves, aspidistra leaf, cypress, New Zealand flax.
Container: Orange trough. (See color plate 20.)

1. The primary stem stands erect in the needle-aid.
2. The "overhanging" aspidistra leaf inclines to the right rear. Under it the "receiving" branch of a strelitzia leaf inclines to the right rear.
3. The long blade of New Zealand flax is added as the "flowing" branch on the lower right. The "waiting" branch of a strelitzia leaf is added on the lower left.
4. The arrangement is completed with additions of the "body" of cypress and the strelitzia flower, the point of which points in the direction of the normal position of the secondary branch.

This is a modern *rikka* and is a free expression of the basic pattern.

1

2

3

1. Material: Pampas, monstera leaf, gladiolus, chrysanthemums, Easter daisy.
   Container: Turquoise trough.

2. Material: Japanese pampas, African feather grass, yellow and white asparagus fern, bleached heads of Japanese pampas, bachelor buttons.
   Container: Terra-cotta vase.

3. Material: Banksia, waratah, dryandra, kangaroo paws, thriptomene.
   Container: Cream ceramic.

4. Material: Many-headed dryandra, dryandra, verticordia, banksia, palm leaf.
   Container: Green ceramic.

4